THE EXECUTIVE BRANCH
OF THE UNITED STATES GOVERNMENT

THE EXECUTIVE BRANCH

OF THE UNITED STATES GOVERNMENT

BY HENRY GILFOND

Blairsville Junior High School
Blairsville, Pennsylvania

Franklin Watts
New York/London/Toronto/Sydney/1981
A First Book

Cover photograph courtesy of: Leo de Wys, Inc.

Photographs courtesy of:
Frontis: United Press International, Inc.;
p. 2: United Press International, Inc.;
p. 6: Independence National Historical Park Collection;
p. 9: New York Public Library Picture Collection;
p. 11: Library of Congress;
p. 19: Franklin D. Roosevelt Library;
p. 22: United Press International, Inc.;
p. 28: New York Public Library Picture Collection;
p. 32: Conklin from Monkmeyer Press Photo Service;
p. 34: United Press International, Inc.;
p. 43: United Press International, Inc.;
p. 47: Conklin from Monkmeyer Press Photo Service;
p. 56: United Press International, Inc.;
p. 59: Conklin from Monkmeyer Press Photo Service.

Diagrams by Vantage Art

Library of Congress Cataloging in Publication Data

Gilfond, Henry.
The executive branch of the United States Government.

(A First Book)
Bibliography: p.
Includes index.
SUMMARY: Discusses the election and official functions of
the President, the nine executive offices of the President,
the Cabinet, departments, and the independent agencies
attached to the executive branch of the government.
1. Presidents—United States—Juvenile literature.
2. United States—Executive departments—
Juvenile literature. [1. Presidents.
2. United States—Executive departments]
I. Title.
JK517.G53   353   80-25729
ISBN 0-531-04251-0

CONTENTS

The Presidency

1

_____

*How the Presidency
Came to Be*

4

_____

Electing the President

7

_____

*War and the
Powers of
the Chief Executive*

16

_____

*Treaties and
the Executive Powers*

20

_____

*The Executive
and Legislation*

23

_____

The White House Staff

29

_____

*Executive Office
of the President*
36

———

The Cabinet
40

———

Departments
45

———

Independent Agencies
53

———

The Vice Presidency
55

———

*Power and
the Presidency*
58

———

For Further Reading
62

———

Index
63

———

To Edythe

THE PRESIDENCY

The President of the United States holds the most powerful office in the country. He is the Chief Executive Officer and Commander in Chief of all the armed forces of the United States. Because the United States is the richest and strongest country in the world, he is also the leader of the Free World and perhaps the most powerful person in the entire globe.

The men who were responsible for establishing the United States would not recognize the country today. The United States has grown from thirteen seaboard states on the Atlantic Ocean into a huge nation of fifty states that spans the North American continent and stretches beyond. Its population, not quite 4 million in 1790, is now more than 203 million.

As the country grew, so did the responsibilities of the President. Since 1790, there have been many different kinds of people, many different kinds of work, many different interests throughout the population. There have been differences of interest between the farmers and the city people, between the producers of cotton and the manufacturers of cotton, between those who worked and those who employed workers in their mills, factories, and mines. Even today there are differences, for example, between chemical manufacturers and conservationists.

The President has responsibilities for the welfare of all these different people. He is held responsible for the economic growth of the country, for the health of the country, for fair relationships between labor and capital, for fair treatment of women and minorities, for education in the country, and much more.

In the 1790s, when the country was much smaller, the Executive Branch could manage its responsibilities with very few

*President-elect Ronald Reagan and his wife Nancy
accept congratulations on Election night, 1980.*

people. Over the years, the Executive Branch has grown into a body of thirteen separate departments. Each department, such as the Department of State, Department of Justice, Department of Agriculture, and the Department of Labor, has developed its own huge bureaucracy.

The size of the country and the great variety of interests—even conflicting interests—among its people made it necessary for the President to delegate responsibilities and authority to the men and women on his personal staff as well as to the heads of the different departments of the Executive Branch of the Government. Of course, the President is ultimately responsible for all actions of this Executive Branch, and some Presidents have tried to maintain complete control of their aides. Such control is an impossible task. The mere size of the bureaucracy does not allow it.

The best the President can do is to surround himself with intelligent and capable men and women to serve as analysts, advisers, and administrators. Finding such people is not always an easy job, but with the huge responsibilities of his office, the President can hardly do less.

With the responsibilities, of course, comes the power. It is the President who establishes and carries on the country's relationships with other countries. He nominates all heads of departments, including the Attorney General. When there is a vacancy on the Supreme Court, the President is responsible for nominating a replacement. He does not establish wage and price controls, but he strongly influences both the cost of goods and the wages of workers. He speaks for the country in all affairs, domestic and foreign. He sets the mood of the country, as Franklin D. Roosevelt did when, in 1932, he changed the whole feeling in the country from that of defeat because of the Great Depression to that of hope. He sets a moral tone not only for the country but for the entire world, as Jimmy Carter did with his human rights campaign, or with his economic boycott of Iran because of its terrorist holding of American hostages, or his boycott of the Moscow Olympics in 1980 because of the Soviet Union's invasion of Afghanistan.

The responsibilities of the President of the United States are great. They may be matched only by the powers of his office.

HOW THE PRESIDENCY CAME TO BE

The Founding Fathers of the newly born United States labored through the spring and summer of 1787 in Philadelphia, framing a constitution that would create a single, united country out of the thirteen original colonies. They needed to revise the existing Articles of Confederation, which gave a certain degree of unity to the country, but did not grapple with the problem of leadership.

It was not an easy job. These people had an especially difficult time creating the office of the presidency, the person who would be the Chief Executive of the Government. Just how was the President to be chosen? For how long was he to hold his office? More important, what powers should be granted the President, and how were these powers to be limited?

Some of the delegates at this Constitutional Convention wanted a president with almost unlimited powers to rule the country. Some, though not many, thought that the new country should be ruled by a king, as George III ruled in England.

There was even one rumor that the Convention was sending for Frederick Augustus, Duke of York and second son of George III. He would be crowned king of the United States!

[4]

Alexander Hamilton, who was to become America's first Secretary of the Treasury, fanned the rumors by making a five-hour speech at the Convention urging the establishment of a monarchy.

The New Jersey delegates to the Constitutional Convention proposed that the Executive Branch of the Government consist of a committee of men, instead of a single person. They also proposed that this executive committee could be ousted from office by a congressional vote.

The Convention rejected both Hamilton's argument for a king and New Jersey's proposal for a committee executive. What the Founding Fathers wisely wanted was a leader the country would respect and esteem. They wanted to endow the president with the power to act as Chief Executive of the country but not the power to act as the *sole* authority. They wanted an executive who would have independence of action, but they wanted definite limits to that independence.

The delegates at the Convention resolved their problem by creating a government with three branches: executive, legislative, and judicial. Each branch was given its own functions, making for a balanced organization: Congress, the Legislative Branch, would make the laws; the Supreme Court, as the Judicial Branch, would study and interpret the laws; and, as head of the Executive Branch, the President would execute the laws. And each branch would serve as a check on the actions of the others. The most important powers of the President, for example, had to meet with the approval of two-thirds of the Senate. The Supreme Court was empowered to rule on legislation enacted by Congress. The President had the power to appoint justices to the Supreme Court, but only with the advice and consent of a two-thirds vote in the Senate. It was to be a government of checks and balances, and, with only a few changes,

The Constitutional Convention was held in 1787 in this room of the State House in Philadelphia.

the process has remained the same for almost two hundred years.

The final framing of the Constitution was the result of much compromise, and very few of the delegates at the Constitutional Convention were completely satisfied with it. Still, for whatever faults it contained, this Constitution proved to be a historic document, and it has served as a model for new republics everywhere in the world.

The framers of the Constitution expected the President to do little more than carry out the will of Congress. Although he had the power to veto (refuse to pass) legislation, his veto could be reversed by a two-thirds vote of the legislators. In fact, the Founding Fathers saw the President as a figurehead for the Government of the United States, performing all the functions of a head of state. He would greet foreign delegates and make an occasional speech to Congress, but any real power that his office might carry would be controlled by Congress.

From the inauguration of George Washington, however, Presidents of the United States have assumed powers the Founding Fathers never dreamed of. They have found ways to interpret the Constitution, thereby giving themselves powers that were neither specifically mentioned nor denied in the Constitution. They have even persuaded Congress to grant them powers the Founding Fathers never intended for the Executive Branch of the Government.

ELECTING THE PRESIDENT

There is one area in the Constitution about which there can be no difference of opinion, the method for electing the Chief Executive of the United States. A great deal of space in the Constitution on the presidency is devoted to this process. Everything is spelled out.

> *Each State shall appoint, in such a manner as the Legislature thereof may direct, a number of electors, equal to the whole number of Senators and Representatives to which the State may be entitled in the Congress. . . . The electors shall meet in their respective States and vote by ballot for two persons, of whom one at least shall not be an inhabitant of the same State with themselves. . . .*

The people do not vote directly for the President, but on Election Day, the first Tuesday after the first Monday in November, every four years, they vote for "electors." Each state votes separately for its own electors. Together, all the electors are members of what is called the Electoral College.

Following the general election, on the first Monday after the second Wednesday in December, the "electors" of each state meet in their own state capital. There they cast their votes for the President and Vice President. It is understood that the electors will vote for the persons to whom they have pledged their votes, but they are not legally bound by their pledges. In other words, they may vote for someone other than the one to whom they have pledged a vote, but this has rarely happened.

The ballots of the electors are sent to Congress. There, in the presence of both houses of Congress, on January 6 following the election (unless it is a Sunday), the ballots are opened and counted.

"The person having the greatest number of votes shall be the President," reads the Constitution, "if such a number be a majority. . . ."

*Senate pages (center) bring boxes
containing the Electoral College ballots
through Statuary Hall in the Capitol to be
counted at the opening of Congress in 1937.*

The vote of the electors, or Electoral College, is not to be confused with the popular vote. In 1876, Samuel J. Tilden had a majority of the popular vote, but Rutherford B. Hayes beat him by one ballot in the electoral vote and became President of the United States. Grover Cleveland had the majority popular vote in 1888 but lost the presidency to Benjamin Harrison by 37 electoral votes.

Originally, the person having the second greatest number of electoral votes was declared the Vice President. In 1804, however, the Twelfth Amendment to the Constitution changed that process. Instead of one vote, the electors now cast two separate ballots, one for President, the other for Vice President.

Prior to the Twelfth Amendment, if no candidate received a majority of electoral ballots, the House of Representatives would choose the President and Vice President from among the five candidates with the greatest number of votes. The Congressmen of each state would meet in private session to decide for whom they would vote. Each state, no matter how large or small, was allowed only one vote in this presidential election procedure. In this manner, when both Thomas Jefferson and Aaron Burr received the same number of electoral votes in 1800, the House of Representatives elected Thomas Jefferson President. Today, if no one gets a complete majority, the House votes for the President from one of the three top candidates.

Before he takes his office, at noon on January 20 following his election, the President takes an oath, or makes an affirmation:

I do solemnly swear (or affirm) that I will faithfully execute the office of the Presidency of the United States, and will, to the best of my ability, preserve, protect, and defend the Constitution of the United States.

An early photograph showing
Abraham Lincoln's second inauguration,
on the front steps of the Capitol.

The oath is plain enough, but, almost from the beginning of America's history, the exact meaning of "preserve, protect, and defend the Constitution" has created great debates and mighty struggles between the President and Congress. Every strong President, beginning with Washington, has interpreted the phrase to suit his own purpose, and often in ways never dreamed of by the Founding Fathers.

There are several other items, however, in this section of the Constitution that can have only one interpretation:

1. To be eligible for election to the office, a person must be a natural born citizen of the United States. He must be thirty-five years or older. He must have lived in the United States for at least fourteen years.

2. If a President is removed from office by impeachment, or dies in office, or resigns, or for whatever reason is no longer capable of carrying out the duties of his office, the Vice President becomes the President. If both President and Vice President leave or are forced to leave their offices, Congress has the responsibility for providing an Acting President until the next presidential election takes place.

3. The President is to be paid a salary as long as he is in office, but his salary may not be increased while he holds that office. (The salary of the President today is $200,000 a year. In addition he is provided with a taxable $50,000 a year for expenses and a nontaxable sum not to exceed $100,000 a year for travel expenses. He also has at his disposal private planes and armored limousines.)

4. The President's term in office is four years.

The Constitution has nothing to say about the re-election of a President. Nor did the Founding Fathers put a limit to the number of terms a person could serve as President of the United States. The feeling among the Founding Fathers was that George Washington would serve as President of the country as long as he lived. At least, that is what they wished when they framed the Constitution.

Washington served two terms and felt that was enough. He believed that no man should become firmly entrenched in the office.

Thomas Jefferson was urged to run for a third term as President, but he refused to make the effort. Along with George Washington, he felt he did not want to see one person President of the United States for any great length of time. Between the two, a precedent was set. Though there were some men who dreamed of serving more than two terms as President, it was not until 1940, 136 years after Jefferson's presidency, that Franklin D. Roosevelt broke the tradition. That year he was elected President for a third time.

In 1951, the country saw to it that Roosevelt's feat could not be repeated. The Twenty-second Amendment to the Constitution, ratified in 1951, states that "No person shall be elected to the office of the President more than twice." More than that, any person who "has held the office of President, or acted as President for more than two years of a term to which some other person was elected" cannot be elected to the office of the President more than once.

This took care of any person who might have become President because of the illness, death, or impeachment of the elected President, and had served more than two years in the office.

5. The President "shall be removed from office on impeachment for, and conviction of, treason, bribery, or other high crimes and misdemeanors." The Vice President and all civil officers of the United States are to be removed from office, if proved guilty of these charges.

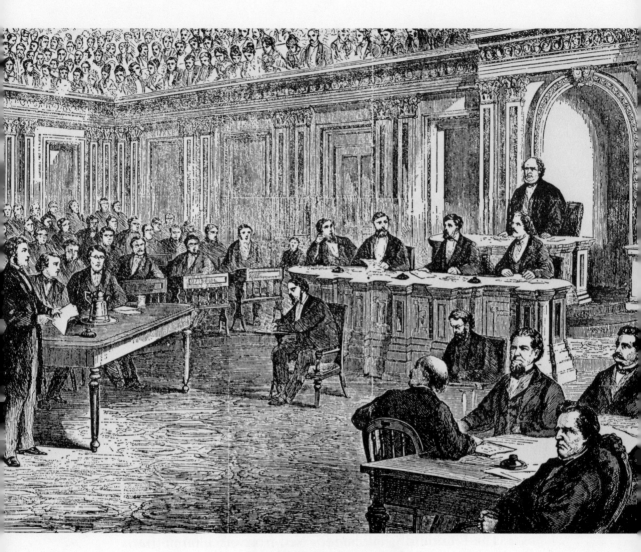

An old print showing the
Senate impeachment trial
of Andrew Johnson.

Only the House of Representatives may impeach the President. That is, the House of Representatives may charge the President with treason, bribery, or other high crimes and misdemeanors. Once charged, or impeached, the President is to be tried by the Senate, with the Chief Justice of the Supreme Court presiding over the trial. A two-thirds vote of the Senate is necessary to bring in a guilty verdict against the President.

Only one President in the history of the United States has ever been impeached, Andrew Johnson, who became President when Abraham Lincoln was assassinated in 1865.

Historians agree that Congress, in a struggle for power, was "out to get" Johnson. When Johnson ordered his Secretary of War, Edwin M. Stanton, to resign in 1868, the House of Representatives saw its opportunity and voted to impeach the President for "high crimes and misdemeanors." Among these accusations was the charge that Johnson used imprudent language and spoke in a loud voice.

Fortunately for Andrew Johnson, if for nobody else, the Senate could not muster the two-thirds majority necessary for conviction. It was a narrow escape, however. The Senate fell just one vote short of finding the President guilty.

Only one other President of the United States has come dangerously close to impeachment, Richard M. Nixon. His actions in the Watergate incident and his cover-up of presidential crimes involved in that incident were not the only presidential criminal acts for which he was about to be impeached. Others involved his responsibility in seeing that laws made by Congress be "faithfully executed." Nixon saved himself from impeachment and certain conviction by resigning the presidency on August 9, 1974. He was the first and, to date, the only President of the United States to resign his office.

WAR AND THE
POWERS OF THE
CHIEF EXECUTIVE

The very first sentence in the Constitution, relating to the presidency, reads: "The executive power shall be vested in the President of the United States of America."

It is the exact meaning and interpretation of "executive power" that has been at the core of the struggle for power between the President and Congress throughout the history of the country.

For example, the Constitution declares: "The President shall be Commander in Chief of the Army and Navy of the United States." It does not give him the power to declare war. That power belongs, constitutionally, to Congress.

Still, in 1793, George Washington declared the United States neutral in the war between Britain and France. It was not a declaration of war, but a declaration related to war; and nowhere does the Constitution give the President the right to make such a declaration.

Abraham Lincoln ignored or broke any number of Constitutional laws to preserve the unity of the country and to defend the Constitution. He enlarged the Army and the Navy without permission of Congress. He spent money without asking Congress to provide those sums. (Congress, alone, is constitutionally empowered to make money available to be spent by the President.)

Lincoln sent warships to blockade Southern ports. He had people arrested without legal warrants and seized property without legal authority. Abraham Lincoln was exercising his interpretation of the "executive power" granted him by the Constitution. He was, he believed, preserving, protecting, and defending the Constitution of the United States.

One hundred years later, John F. Kennedy, without permission of Congress, ordered a naval blockade of Cuba to force the Soviet Union to dismantle its nuclear missile bases on that island. Kennedy did not call his act a blockade, but a "quarantine." It was a blockade, nonetheless, and as such could have caused serious international repercussions.

President Lyndon B. Johnson sent thousands of troops in battle against the North Vietnamese without Congressional authorization to fight a war. Similarly, Richard M. Nixon ordered the bombing of Cambodia without a declaration of war by Congress.

In each case, past and present, when questioned on such actions, the President declared that he was acting in defense of the United States. It is doubtful that this kind of defense is what the Founding Fathers meant when they wrote the Constitution. But this is how a number of strong Presidents of the United States have read and interpreted the Constitution to suit their policies.

Sometimes those policies worked well for the country, as in the actions of Abraham Lincoln and in John F. Kennedy's quarantine of Cuba. At other times, those policies proved costly. Billions of dollars were wasted in Vietnam; thousands of young Americans lost their lives in that action, and many thousands more were wounded and maimed for life.

The public clamor against the war in Vietnam was so great that Congress finally acted to prevent the possibility of further presidential decisions to send troops into combat on foreign soil. In 1973, Congress passed the War Powers Act "to ensure that the collective judgment of both Congress and the President will apply to the introduction of United States armed forces into hostilities."

The Act, referring to the Constitution, held that the President, as Commander in Chief, could send American forces into battle only if there were a declaration of war; or if he were requested to do so by Congress; or if there were an attack upon the United States, its territories or possessions, or its armed forces.

President Nixon vetoed the Act, but Congress overrode his veto and the Act became law.

The War Powers Act, however, has already been bent a little, if not disregarded entirely. Without consulting Congress, President Gerald R. Ford ordered American armed forces to assist in the evacuation of Americans from Da Nang and Saigon in South Vietnam in April and May of 1975.

He sent troops to retake the *Mayaguez,* an American ship seized by Cambodians, and to rescue the crew. Forty-one marines were killed in the mission, and fifty more were wounded. Ironically, the captured crew of the *Mayaguez* had been released and sent to Thailand just half an hour before the rescue squad went into action.

In 1980, Jimmy Carter, without consulting Congress, sent armed forces into Iran to rescue the fifty-three American hostages held by that country. Eight of the rescue team were killed, and helicopters, as well as an air-transport, were lost in the action. The hostages were not freed.

Both Presidents justified their actions. Ford claimed that none of his military actions was contrary to his Constitutional rights as Chief Executive and Commander in Chief. Jimmy Carter asserted that the action he had ordered was a "rescue" mission, not an act of war.

The system of checks and balances at work.
Since the President is not empowered
to do so himself, Franklin D. Roosevelt
asks Congress to declare war on Japan
after the attack on Pearl Harbor.

It is not in the use of armed forces alone that presidents, particularly strong presidents, manipulate the words of the Constitution to suit their aims. Sometimes, the results were helpful to the country and served to preserve the United States and its Constitution. Sometimes, however, the results have been destructive.

Nixon, for example, distorted the intentions and dictates of the Constitution, often disregarding them to such an extent that the credibility of the whole Federal Government was weakened. Once his unconstitutional actions and activities were revealed to the people, it was inevitable that he would be impeached or resign the presidency.

He left his office, probably the most prestigious and powerful political position in the entire world, thoroughly disgraced. He was personally saved from further embarrassment and possible imprisonment only by the presidential pardon that President Ford gave him.

The Constitution gives the President the "power to grant reprieves and pardons for offenses against the United States, except in cases of impeachment." But a great number of people questioned Ford's pardon of Nixon, and that pardon probably lost Ford his election in the 1976 presidential race.

TREATIES AND
THE EXECUTIVE POWERS

The Constitution gives the President the power to appoint ambassadors and to make treaties with foreign countries "with the advice and consent of the Senate, provided two-thirds of the Senators present concur."

In other words, the Constitution requires the President to consult with the Senate before and during treaty negotiations with a foreign power. And two-thirds of the Senators present in the Senate at the time of the vote must ballot to accept the treaty before it becomes binding on the United States.

The President rarely has trouble with the appointment of his ambassadors. He has, however, had considerable difficulty at times making treaties.

The Treaty of Versailles between the allied powers, the United States, and Germany, at the end of World War I, was negotiated by President Woodrow Wilson. But the Senate did not give it the necessary two-thirds vote and the treaty was killed.

The treaty giving back the Panama Canal to Panama was approved by the Senate in 1979 only after years of fierce opposition.

President Jimmy Carter, who negotiated and signed the second Strategic Arms Limitation Treaty (SALT II) with the Soviet Union in Vienna, June 18, 1979, never submitted that treaty to the Senate for approval. There was so much opposition to it in the Senate that the President was waiting for a time when he could be more sure of the needed two-thirds vote.

More important, Presidents have avoided the difficulties of treaty-making by reaching executive agreements with foreign nations. These agreements do not need the approval of the Senate. There is nothing in the Constitution that gives the President the right to make such agreements or that specifically prevents him from doing so. He executes them on the grounds that he is the Chief Executive and Commander in Chief.

In 1817, President James Monroe made an agreement with Britain, limiting naval forces on the Great Lakes. President William McKinley laid down the terms for the ending of the

President Richard M. Nixon heads across
the Oval Office to accept the
credentials of unseen foreign ambassadors.
The Presidential seal, in the foreground,
is woven into the rug.

Spanish-American War by executive agreement, although the Senate later ratified these terms. In 1905, President Theodore Roosevelt, in a secret executive agreement with Japan, approved a Japanese military occupation of Korea. This agreement remained secret for twenty years before it was discovered in Roosevelt's private papers.

The Armistice that stopped the fighting in World War I, the recognition of the Soviet Union in 1933, the agreement to occupy and defend Iceland in 1941, the Atlantic Charter of 1941, and the agreements to end World War II are all examples of executive agreements that bypassed the treaty procedure that demands a two-thirds confirmation by the U.S. Senate.

The Constitution states, simply, that the President "shall receive ambassadors and other public ministers." As some of the Founding Fathers saw this, the receiving of ambassadors from foreign nations was to be no more than a social function.

It later developed that when a President received representatives of foreign countries, he was, in effect, giving recognition to the government of that country. Congress may pass resolutions urging the President to recognize or not recognize a new government or nation, but the power of recognition and the establishment of diplomatic relations with other countries remains the President's right and power.

THE EXECUTIVE AND LEGISLATION

The President, from time to time, delivers a speech to Congress on the state of the Union, and the President recommends legislation. These are duties of the office, as stated in the Constitution. He must also see to it that the Constitution and the laws passed by Congress are "faithfully executed."

One of the President's jobs:
here, in the twenties,
Warren G. Harding reads
his annual message to Congress.

It is in the executing of the law that Presidents have sometimes been less than cooperative.

When Congress allocates a sum of money to be spent by the Government for a specific purpose, and this is a right belonging only to Congress, it is the duty of the President to spend that money for the specific purpose.

But Thomas Jefferson, in 1803, refused to spend the money Congress had voted for the building of gunboats. Withholding this kind of money is called impoundment. Ulysses S. Grant impounded money voted for river and harbor funds. Franklin D. Roosevelt impounded part of the funds voted for public works. Harry S. Truman impounded funds voted for the Air Force. No President, however, denied the will of Congress by impounding more funds more often than Richard Nixon did.

By 1973, Nixon had impounded about $15 billion. This was almost 20 percent of the money Congress had voted for a variety of Federal programs. More than a hundred such programs suffered for these impoundments. Nixon's impoundment policy amounted to an attempt on his part to nullify a Constitutional right of Congress, the power to appropriate funds for federal expenditure.

Nixon tried further to limit the powers of Congress by declaring that he would enforce certain parts of Congressional legislation and not enforce others. Specifically, he declared that he would not enforce part of the Civil Rights Act of 1964. He failed in his effort to weaken the powers of Congress when the Court of Appeals ruled that he must enforce every section of the Act.

In 1973, Nixon attempted to destroy the Office of Economic Opportunity, a Congressional committee. He did this by simply cutting out of his budget all funds for the committee. However, the courts came to the rescue of the Constitution once more. They ruled that the President was exercising a veto power not granted by the Constitution.

A third assault on the powers of Congress was Nixon's use of what is called a pocket veto.

Constitutionally, the President must sign any legislation by Congress to make it a law of the country. If he does not return the legislation signed to Congress within ten days after he has received it, the legislation "shall be a law, in like manner, as if he had signed it." Only if Congress adjourns before the ten days given the President to return the legislation signed does the legislation die, that is, it does not become law.

Nixon did not wait for Congress to adjourn to pocket veto the Family Practice of Medicine Act. This Act, authorizing grants of $225 million to hospitals and medical schools, was passed almost unanimously by Congress. However, two days before the legislation was to be returned to Congress, signed or vetoed, Congress took its traditional five-day Christmas break. Nixon treated the "break" as if it were the adjournment at the end of a Congressional session. On December 24, he announced a pocket veto of the bill. This was an absolute veto and Congress could not override it. Eventually, this Nixon pocket veto was declared unconstitutional in the courts.

Another effort on the part of Nixon to limit the powers of Congress came in his attempt to appoint a justice to the Supreme Court. He actually wrote in a letter to a Senator that the Constitution gave him and only him this power. He conveniently forgot or ignored the fact that the Constitution gives him no more than the right to nominate a justice with the advice of the Senate and to appoint a justice with the consent of the Senate.

In addition to his attacks on the rights of Congress, Nixon invoked the right of executive privilege as no other President in the past or since has done. Executive privilege has been employed by Presidents, from the earliest days, to refuse to deliver papers, documents, or other materials to Congress, when Congress asked for them.

Neither Presidents Kennedy nor Lyndon B. Johnson employed executive privilege, but Nixon invoked it four times in his first term as President. Members of his administration refused to testify before, or hand over documents to, Congress twenty-three times. At the beginning of his second term, Nixon declared that every member of the White House staff, past or present, could refuse to give testimony or deliver documents to any Congressional committee. By May of 1973, he announced that his staff could refuse to answer questions asked by grand juries and even by the Federal Bureau of Investigation (FBI).

In this way Nixon was able to conceal from both Congress and the rest of the nation burglaries, illegal wire taps, secret bombing raids, the illegal work of his White House investigating squads called "plumbers," his private "enemies list," and other such crimes and misdemeanors.

In fact, Congress had been losing its authority for a long time, and largely by its own doing. Over the years, Congress had given the President almost full control of the government bureaucracy. They had passed some 500 laws giving the President the power to take extraordinary executive action in case of emergency or in case of "public peril."

Under these laws, in wartime for example, the President may allocate the civilian labor force and industrial materials; control imports and exports, excess profits, and internal and international communications; seize plants for war production; regulate labor relations; impose wage and price controls and censorship; and imprison people considered as security risks.

Franklin D. Roosevelt used some of these powers when he

On August 14, 1935,
Franklin D. Roosevelt signed the
Social Security Act,
thus giving the Act its final authority.

became President during the depression of the 1930s. Congress was little more than a rubber stamp in those days, approving every measure Roosevelt proposed in an effort to get the country back on its economic feet. Less admirable was the executive order to intern Japanese citizens into what amounted to concentration camps in the first years of World War II.

To put a check on the mounting powers of the President and to regain some of its own power, Congress passed the National Emergencies Act in 1976. The Act cut down the number of reasons the President might give for announcing a state of emergency. The Act abolished most of the emergency laws that had been in effect, and it set a limit of one year on any state of emergency the President might declare. The state of emergency could be renewed only if the President gave Congress notice of his desire to continue it. In any case, Congress must vote to continue the state of emergency every six months. And, finally, Congress can call off the state of emergency at any time by a simple majority vote in both Houses.

THE WHITE HOUSE STAFF

George Washington's White House staff consisted of just two people. One was his nephew, and the other had been an aide to the General during the Revolutionary War. Washington had to pay for his assistants out of his own pocket. It was not until William McKinley became President in 1897 that Congress voted salaries for the White House staff, and it was only in 1939 that Congress gave the President the right to hire administrative assistants.

[29]

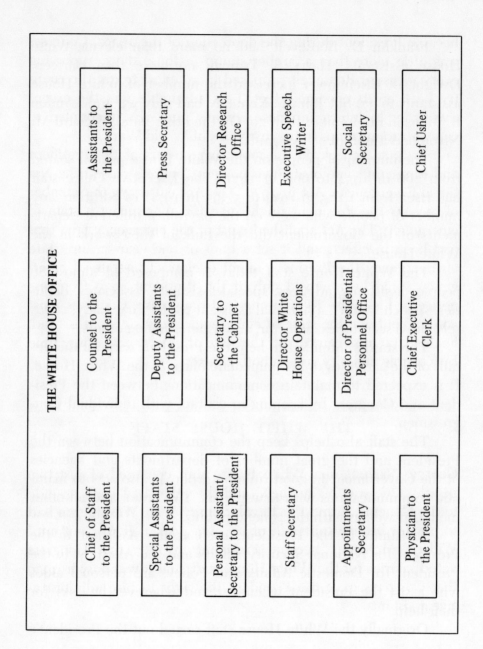

THE WHITE HOUSE OFFICE

Chief of Staff to the President	Counsel to the President	Assistants to the President
Special Assistants to the President	Deputy Assistants to the President	Press Secretary
Personal Assistant/Secretary to the President	Secretary to the Cabinet	Director Research Office
Staff Secretary	Director White House Operations	Executive Speech Writer
Appointments Secretary	Director of Presidential Personnel Office	Social Secretary
Physician to the President	Chief Executive Clerk	Chief Usher

Franklin D. Roosevelt had no more than eleven White House assistants, Harry S. Truman no more than thirteen. Dwight D. Eisenhower increased the number of White House assistants to 37, but John F. Kennedy had only 23, and Lyndon B. Johnson rarely more than 20. On the other hand, Richard M. Nixon had a staff of 48 assistants.

The number of people on the White House payroll soared from 266 in 1954 to 600 in 1971. The Executive Office staff had risen from 1,175 in 1954 to 5,395 in 1971. In addition, any number of people who were on the payroll of different departments of the Government did the bulk of their work in the White House.

The White House staff today is composed of almost 80 people: assistants, advisers, special assistants, associates, deputies, speech writers, a personal assistant to the First Lady, counsels, press secretaries, a doctor, and ushers, among others.

The staff is intended to help the President with all the details of the activities of his immediate office in the White House. It is expected to maintain communications between the President and Congress by keeping in contact with individual Congressmen.

The staff also helps keep the communication between the President and the great number of departments and agencies of the Government in good running order. It also acts to maintain communications with newspapers, TV, radio, and all other media, as well as with the general public.

Assistants to the President, such as the Assistant to the President for National Security Affairs and the Assistant to the President for Domestic Affairs and Policy, are personal aides who assist the President whenever and wherever he asks for their help.

Originally the White House staff sorted out the President's

*President Jimmy Carter answers
questions at a Press Conference held in
the East Room of the White House.*

mail, paid the servants, took care of the Chief Executive's private accounts, made arrangements for state dinners, and such. All this is still done by members of the White House staff. But it does much more today and, in a number of cases, has developed considerable power on its own.

Members of the White House staff can act as chairpersons at interdepartmental committee meetings. They draft speeches to be made by political executives. They read speeches the executives are about to deliver to make sure that they fit in with the policies of the President. When a critical moment arises, they will take control of an agency. They will take over a job that normally belongs to an ambassador and travel to foreign countries as representatives of the President and the United States.

It was generally accepted that Henry Kissinger, who was Richard Nixon's Assistant to the President for National Security Affairs during his first term in office, was more powerful than the Secretary of State, Dean Rusk. Kissinger's power lessened the authority of the State Department, and foreign diplomats wanted to see him, not the Secretary, for meaningful talks and decisions.

John Ehrlichman and H. R. Haldeman, who headed the White House staff under President Nixon, were more powerful than any of the heads of the domestic executive departments. Haldeman and Ehrlichman were called "the palace guard." No one could see the President, or even get a note to him, without approval from either or both of these White House staffers.

It is true that any President has an enormously busy schedule and that his aides should relieve him of problems that can be solved by others. But the judgment of aides can isolate the

In the Lincoln Room of the White House,
Richard M. Nixon and Henry Kissinger,
the man who became his Secretary of State,
discuss foreign policy in 1973.

President from what might prove to be very important information and the need to make critical decisions.

For example, a White House counsel and his staff knew that there was a report by the comptroller of currency that charged Bert Lance with "inappropriate action" as a banker. President Jimmy Carter had made Bert Lance Director of the Office of Management and Budget. But no one on the White House staff informed Carter of the charges against Lance. Bert Lance had to resign his office, and Jimmy Carter's credibility suffered for it.

Often enough, the White House staff gets into trouble on its own. There was strong feeling that Dwight D. Eisenhower should dismiss the top man on his staff, Sherman Adams, when it was disclosed that he had accepted gifts from an industrialist. The press, as well as Congress and everyone else who works for the Government, has little love for the members of the White House staff.

The President does not need Congressional approval of his appointments to the White House staff, as he does with his appointments to heads of departments. As a result, it has been customary for Presidents to staff the White House with loyal friends. Lyndon B. Johnson's most important staff members were people from his home state, Texas, and Nixon's staff was made up largely of California businessmen. President Ford filled his staff with people from his home state, Michigan. And Jimmy Carter gave the more important jobs on the White House staff to his fellow Georgians.

It is quite normal for the President to surround himself with loyal advisers. It is a far cry, however, from the practice of early Presidents, who sought out brilliant men of opposing opinions for their advisers.

EXECUTIVE OFFICE
OF THE PRESIDENT

Office of
Management and Budget

There are nine Executive Offices of the President, Government organizations directly responsible to the Chief Executive. None is more powerful than the *Office of Management and Budget (OMB)*. The Director of the OMB is as powerful as any member of the President's Cabinet, and more powerful than most.

The OMB was created: (1) to develop and maintain the structure and procedures of the Executive Branch of the Government; (2) to help develop the mechanics of government and the way it works; (3) to help the President prepare his budget; (4) to supervise and control the way the money in the President's budget is spent; (5) to keep the President informed of the activities of the different government departments and agencies, the work they propose to do, the work they are doing, and the work they have completed.

The most important responsibility of the OMB, however, is concerned with Congressional legislation. And here, the OMB exercises its great powers.

Whenever legislation is introduced in Congress, OMB gets the opinion and advice of many government agencies and departments that might be affected by the particular piece of legislation introduced. Sometimes it will get those opinions and advice before the legislation is actually introduced. It coordinates all those opinions and advice and delivers the results to the President, generally with its own opinion on the proposed legislation. There are times when the OMB director will inform Congress that a particular piece of legislation will not meet with

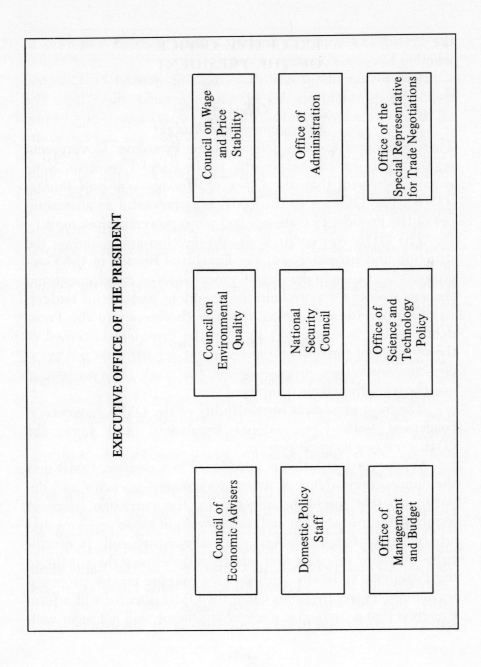

EXECUTIVE OFFICE OF THE PRESIDENT

Council of Economic Advisers

Domestic Policy Staff

Office of Management and Budget

Council on Environmental Quality

National Security Council

Office of Science and Technology Policy

Council on Wage and Price Stability

Office of Administration

Office of the Special Representative for Trade Negotiations

the President's approval, and that the President will veto it, whether Congress passes it or not.

Every year about one thousand bills passed by Congress go to the President for his signature to make them law. The OMB saves the President much time by recommending to him that he give his signature or his veto. Within five days after the President gets a Congressional bill on his desk, the OMB is required to present its comments and opinion on the bill. When it recommends the President's signature, the bill is almost always approved by the President.

With this kind of power resting with the OMB, it can be clearly understood why the Senate insists on its right to approve or disapprove the President's nomination for the post of Director of the Office of Management and Budget, by the normal two-thirds vote.

National Security Council

The members of this Executive Office of the President include the President, Vice President, Secretary of State, and Secretary of Defense. Its advisers include the Director of the Central Intelligence Agency (CIA), and the Chairman of the Joint Chiefs of Staff (armed forces). Officials in this office are the President's Assistant for National Security Affairs, the Deputy Assistant, and a staff secretary.

The responsibility of the *National Security Council* is to advise the President on matters dealing with the integration of domestic, foreign, and military policies relating to national security. For the most part, however, the President does not give the Council much of his time. Carter reduced the National Security Council staff and turned it into a "think tank," an organization that did little more than discuss problems related to national security and turn in the results of its discussions.

[38]

The Central Intelligence Agency (CIA) is responsible for gathering and evaluating foreign intelligence. It conducts counter-intelligence outside the United States and works secretly to bring about changes in foreign nations, changes that will prove beneficial to the national security of the United States.

Through its covert actions it helped overthrow the government in Iran, in 1953, in Guatemala in 1954, and in Indonesia in 1958. It can also help to install new governments, as it did in Syria in 1954 and in Laos in 1959.

Sometimes the covert actions of the CIA are less than successful. It organized the invasion in 1960 and 1961 of the Bay of Pigs by Cuban refugees from the Castro government. The invasion proved to be a complete failure and served only to strengthen Castro's position in Cuba.

The CIA is also responsible for counter-intelligence in the United States, cooperating with the Federal Bureau of Investigation (FBI). It was this work, particularly in the Watergate scandals, that created a great deal of difficulty for the CIA and accounts for the present problems of the organization. The CIA lost the respect of the American people and, with it, suffered a drastic cut in staff and funds. Congress voted that the CIA must report to the Government not only on its ongoing activities but also on any important activities it is planning.

Other Executive Offices

The Council of Economic Advisers analyzes the national economy and keeps the President informed on national economic developments. It evaluates economic programs of the Government, and recommends economic programs as well.

The Domestic Policy Staff formulates and coordinates domestic policy. It evaluates the needs of the country, gives the

President its advice on domestic issues, and recommends domestic policies to the Chief Executive.

The Office of the Special Representative for Trade Negotiations is responsible for supervising trade agreements with foreign countries and taking part in shaping trade agreements with foreign nations.

The Council of Environmental Quality, which has been particularly busy in recent years, analyzes the changes or trends in the national environment, and evaluates the Government's environmental programs. It also conducts studies of the environment, which include the effects of nuclear plants and nuclear-waste disposal.

The Council on Wage and Price Stability keeps its eyes on wages, costs, productivity, profits, and prices. It also evaluates the programs, policies, and activities of all other Government departments and agencies to see how they affect inflation.

The Office of Science and Technology Policy advises the President on how scientific and technological developments affect the economy, national security, health, foreign relations, and the environment of the country.

The Office of Administration provides all executive offices of the President with whatever information and other services they may seek: data processing, library services, general office operation, printing, mail, messengers, and office supplies.

THE CABINET

The Cabinet is made up of the heads of the thirteen executive departments: the Secretaries of Agriculture, Commerce, De-

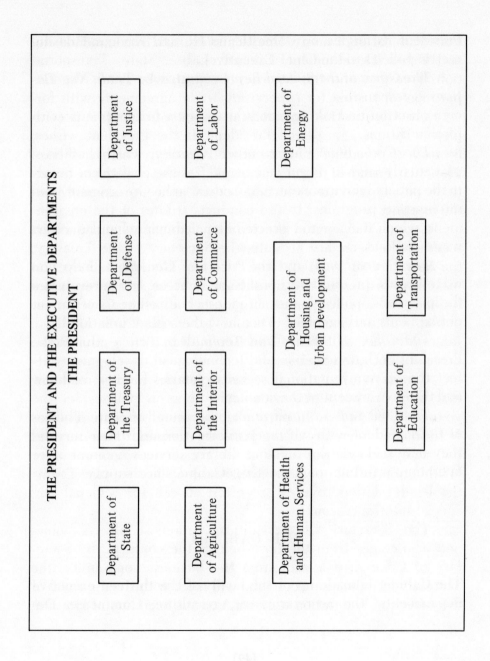

THE PRESIDENT AND THE EXECUTIVE DEPARTMENTS

THE PRESIDENT

Department of Justice

Department of Labor

Department of Energy

Department of Defense

Department of Commerce

Department of Housing and Urban Development

Department of Transportation

Department of the Treasury

Department of the Interior

Department of Education

Department of State

Department of Agriculture

Department of Health and Human Services

fense, Education, Energy, Health and Human Services, Housing and Urban Development, Interior, Labor, State, Transportation, Treasury, and the Attorney General, who heads the Department of Justice.

The Constitution says nothing about a Cabinet; it is completely the creation of the President. If the President wishes, he may give Cabinet rank to other Executive Branch officials. The Vice President is present at all Cabinet meetings. Sometimes people who are experts in special areas are asked to join the meetings.

George Washington created the Cabinet when he called together the Secretary of State, the Secretary of the Treasury, the Secretary of War, and the Attorney General to help him make his presidential decisions. Each of these secretaries was a brilliant and forceful person. In fact, in the first years of the republic, Cabinet members Thomas Jefferson, James Madison, James Monroe, and Martin Van Buren all in turn became Presidents of the United States.

George Washington chose his secretaries because he knew that they did not agree with each other on policies for the young United States. In particular, Secretary of State Thomas Jefferson and Secretary of the Treasury Alexander Hamilton did not see eye to eye. But many of the Presidents who came after Washington did not organize their Cabinets in this way. Today, the heads of departments are often chosen for regional and special-interest reasons.

The Secretary of Agriculture is almost always someone who comes from the farm-belt of the country, the Secretary of Commerce a man from the business community, the Secretary of Labor someone who will meet with the approval of the American Federation of Labor, and the Secretary of Housing

**A 1979 photo showing
President Carter and his Cabinet
meeting at the White House.**

and Urban Development a distinguished person with ties to minority groups in the country.

At times these appointments have proved disastrous. President Warren G. Harding gave the post of Secretary of the Interior to one of his political friends, Albert B. Fall. Fall was charged with conspiracy and bribery in the Teapot Dome scandal, which involved the fraudulent leasing of naval oil reserves, and went to jail.

The Cabinets of the first Presidents of the country were small and their discussions of national policy, both domestic and foreign, were meaningful. Today, with so many heads of the different departments meeting in Cabinet sessions, each with their particular problems and interests, the meetings are not very fruitful. Each department secretary prefers to explore individual problems and to come to decisions with the President alone. There is little of common interest between the Secretary of State and the Secretary of Housing and Urban Development, for example. Both learn more and get more accomplished in meetings outside the formal Cabinet sessions.

As a matter of fact, there are few full Cabinet meetings. Kennedy did not attend many meetings of the Cabinet in his three years as President, and Nixon hardly ever attended Cabinet meetings. Lyndon B. Johnson went to these meetings to discuss problems that were bothering him, not to hear the Cabinet's opinions and problems.

Andrew Jackson, for all practical purposes, ignored the Cabinet. When he had to resolve important problems or make important decisions, he discussed matters with his old friends, who came to be called the "Kitchen Cabinet." Franklin D. Roosevelt had his "Brain Trust," Kennedy his "Irish Mafia." Nixon relied heavily, particularly in foreign affairs, on one man, Henry Kissinger.

DEPARTMENTS

Department of State

The State Department is perhaps the most important of all Executive Offices. The Secretary of State is, traditionally, the principal foreign policy adviser to the President. He is responsible for the direction of U.S. foreign policy and supervises U.S. foreign relations. He is responsible for the Foreign Service in all parts of the world and for all diplomatic missions and delegations to international organizations. Ambassadors, appointed by the President, report to the President through the Secretary of State.

Presidents, for one reason or another, have cut down the role of the State Department, and particularly that of the Secretary of State. In earlier times the President had good reason to suspect the Secretary of State of political ambitions, of aiming for the presidency itself. Abraham Lincoln had considerable trouble with his ambitious Secretary of State William H. Seward, and many Presidents have installed weaker men as Secretaries of State because they wished to run the State Department themselves.

Franklin D. Roosevelt had a gentle man, Cordell Hull, for his Secretary of State, but, whether he asked others for advice or not, Roosevelt conducted American foreign policy almost completely as he saw fit. Nixon had the quiet William Rogers for his Secretary of State but liked to think he was making American policy with only the aid of his Assistant for National Security Affairs, Henry Kissinger.

Other Presidents have chosen men with outstanding qualities for this most important post: Washington had Jefferson, Jefferson had Madison, Madison had Monroe. In more recent times, Theodore Roosevelt had two excellent men as Secretary of State, John Hay and Elihu Root. Harding did not have a brilliant presidency, but he had a brilliant man as his Secretary of State, Charles Evans Hughes. Eisenhower had John Foster Dulles, and Truman had, among others, George Marshall.

Jimmy Carter had a man of great reputation as his Secretary of State, Cyrus Vance, but he also had another strong man as Assistant to the President for National Security Affairs, Zbigniew Brzezinski. There were some who were not sure who ran foreign policy for the country, Vance or Brzezinski. Vance resigned because he opposed Carter's sending an armed "rescue mission" into Iran, and he was replaced in 1980 by Edmund S. Muskie. Whatever the case, Carter himself was extremely active in the foreign policy scene. He helped engineer the peace between Egypt and Israel, where Nixon and Kissinger had failed. He pushed through the treaty which will give the Panama Canal back to Panama. He led the world in its efforts to get the Soviets to withdraw their troops from Afghanistan. He pressured many countries of the Free World to boycott Iran in an effort to free the American hostages held by that country.

The part played by either the Secretary of State or Brzezinski, or both, in these foreign affairs has not been disclosed. International negotiations are still kept rather secret by both the President and the State Department.

Department of Defense

This department is responsible for providing the military forces needed to deter war and protect the security of the nation. These forces include about two million men and women on active duty in the Army, Navy, Marine Corps, and Air Force; 50,000 ships at sea; and two and a half million men and women in reserve units. About one million civilians are employed by the Defense Department.

While President Carter watches,
Edmund S. Muskie is sworn in
as Secretary of State in May 1980.

The Secretary of Defense is head of the department that includes the separately organized Army, Navy, and Air Force Departments, as well as the Chairman of the Joint Chiefs of Staff of the Armed Forces. Among its many agencies are the Defense Civil Preparedness Agency, the Defense Investigative Service for criminal investigation and crime prevention, and the Defense Nuclear Agency that developed the first atomic bomb.

Department of Justice

This department, headed generally by the Attorney General, is responsible for enforcing the laws of the land. It has thousands of agents, investigators, and lawyers whose job is to protect the people against criminals and subversive actions, actions aimed to destroy the Constitution and the nation. It has the duty to ensure healthy business competition in our system of free enterprise. It also enforces drug laws, and immigration and naturalization laws. Its other duties include law enforcement, crime prevention, crime detection and prosecution, and rehabilitation of drug-users and other offenders of the law.

In addition, the Attorney General directs and supervises the activities of U.S. attorneys and marshals throughout the country.

Among the various divisions of the Department of Justice none is better known than the Federal Bureau of Investigation (FBI). The FBI gathers facts, locates witnesses, and prepares evidence in matters in which the Federal Government may be interested. This covers a wide area that includes, among other things, espionage, sabotage, kidnaping, extortion, bank robbery, civil rights violations, and assassination of the President.

The record of the FBI in tracking down criminals of all sorts has made a legend of the organization, and it has been one of the most highly respected agencies of the government. Its

[48]

long-time director, J. Edgar Hoover, was a living legend. He was one of the most admired and feared men in the country; no President dared to relieve him of his post. To the credit of the FBI, Richard Nixon could not get Hoover to call off the FBI's investigation of the Watergate burglary.

However, not everything the FBI did under Hoover was to be admired or applauded. Hoover had files on everyone he considered un-American. The files included people in the civil rights movement and the movement against the Vietnam War, respected people whose patriotism could not be questioned. It was revealed in Congress that Hoover withheld important information on the assassination of John Kennedy from the Warren Commission when it was investigating the killing of the President.

Because of these discoveries and the FBI's lack of cooperation in the Watergate hearings (after the death of J. Edgar Hoover), the FBI's reputation was tarnished, and there was a Congressional effort to reduce its powers.

More recently, the FBI began an investigation that, at first, was an effort to track down art thieves. It wound up by discovering that it was possible to bribe Congressmen, among others.

But even here, the FBI faltered. There were "leaks" to the press before its investigation was completed, alleging that a number of Congressmen had accepted bribes from the FBI (posing as rich Arabs) for promised political favors. Guilty or not, these Congressmen, and others, had their reputations smeared.

People wanted to know whether the FBI had leaked the stories. They even wanted to know whether the FBI had the moral right to attempt to bribe elected representatives of the people for any reason. And the Arabs, cast in the roles of evil lawbreakers, were not pleased, either.

Congress knows that the country needs a Federal Bureau

of Investigation, but it wants an FBI that is free of any criminal intention or action.

Department of the Treasury

The Department of Treasury is perhaps best known among the American people for one of its bureaus, the Internal Revenue Service, which collects income tax for the Federal Government. Headed by the Secretary of the Treasury, the department has other responsibilities as well. It recommends economic, financial, and tax policies to the President, collects duties on goods imported into the country, and checks the operations of national banks. Its Bureau of Alcohol, Tobacco, and Firearms is responsible for seeing that Federal regulations in these areas are not broken. Its Bureau of Engraving and Printing produces paper currency, Treasury bonds and bills, postage stamps, and revenue stamps. Its Bureau of the Mint produces the country's coins as well as medals for special occasions. The department is also responsible for selling and redeeming U.S. Saving Bonds.

A very important branch of the Department of the Treasury is the U.S. Secret Service. The duty of the Secret Service is to detect and arrest forgers of coins or currency. Perhaps its more important duty, and certainly the one for which it is best known, is protecting the lives of the President and the Vice President and their families. The Secret Service also protects candidates for the presidency in election years; former Presidents and their wives, as long as they live; widows of former Presidents as long as they live or until they remarry; children of former Presidents until they become sixteen years old; and the Presidents-elect and Vice Presidents-elect.

The Secret Service is also charged with the protection of visiting heads of state: kings, queens, presidents of foreign countries, prime ministers, and the like.

Department of Agriculture

The work of this department, under the Secretary of Agriculture, is to improve and maintain farm income and to develop foreign markets for U.S. farm products. It helps landowners protect their soil and water and is responsible for the country's forests and other natural resources. It is also responsible for the country's daily food supply, and it inspects and grades this food to ensure that it meets standard quality. Through a number of programs, the department helps fight poverty, hunger, and malnutrition. For example, it sees that children get nutritious and inexpensive lunches in their schools.

Department of Commerce

This department, with the Secretary of Commerce at its head, promotes national economic development. It also promotes technological advancement and assists in the development of the U.S. merchant marine. It is in charge of patents for inventions and protects trademarks for the business community. The Bureau of the Census is an important branch of the Commerce Department.

Department of Energy

The energy crisis makes this department particularly important to the American people. This department promotes conservation programs and programs to develop other sources for the energy the country needs, such as solar energy, clean coal energy, water energy, and wind energy. The department also sets the rates and charges for energy fuels, natural gas, electricity, and hydraulic power.

Oddly perhaps, the department also monitors and reviews all matters related to civil rights and equal opportunity in the labor market.

Department of Health
and Human Services

This is the executive department that is most concerned with people's everyday needs. It makes health services available to as many people as possible. It administers the Social Security program and protects the health of the nation with the Food and Drug Administration that bans impure food, drugs, cosmetics, and other hazards to life. Medicare and Medicaid are also the responsibilities of this department as is the enforcement of laws dealing with child support.

Department of Housing
and Urban Development

As its title indicates, this department's mission is to help develop housing for the people—especially the poorer people—of the country. Its work has had some effect on improvements in urban and suburban communities, particularly in the inner cities of large metropolitan areas. The delivery of aid to so-called disaster areas that have been devastated by fires, floods, hurricanes, and other natural causes is part of the job of this department.

Department of the Interior

This department is responsible for public lands and natural resources. It protects national parks and historical places and provides recreation areas for the people of the country. It is also responsible for the social and economic development of U.S. territories and programs for American Indians and the people native to Alaska.

Department of Labor

This department was set up to promote and develop the welfare of American working people, improve working conditions and to help create job possibilities. It directs the collection of statistics concerning labor conditions. It enforces laws covering maximum hours of work, minimum wages, child labor, and safety and health standards in working places. It provides labor-management services and encourages the practice of job-training programs throughout the country.

Department of Transportation

Highway planning and construction, railroads, aviation, and urban mass transit are all responsibilities of this department. So are ports, the safety of waterways, highways, and oil and gas lines. The U.S. Coast Guard is under the supervision of this department.

Department of Education

This is the newest department in the Executive Branch of the government. Once part of the Department of Health and Human Services (previously known as Health, Education, and Welfare), it was established September 27, 1979. Its responsibility, obviously, is the education of the American people. President Carter argued that such responsibility demanded a separate executive department and Congress, whose vote was necessary for the creation of the department, agreed with him.

INDEPENDENT AGENCIES

There are about fifty independent agencies attached to the Executive Branch of the U.S. Government. They are involved with everything from consumer products to the administration of the Tennessee Valley Authority, from farm credits to overseeing equal job opportunity, from environmental protection to the care of American battle monuments.

[53]

For example, there is ACTION that mobilizes such voluntary services as the Peace Corps for volunteer help to underdeveloped countries and VISTA (Volunteers in Service to America) for volunteer work among the underprivileged in the United States. RSVP (Retired Senior Volunteer Program) encourages retired people to volunteer their help to entire communities.

The Commission on Civil Rights promotes and regulates equal rights, and the Equal Employment Opportunity Commission helps settle problems in equal rights disputes in the job market.

The Federal Deposit Insurance Corporation insures national banks and state banks that are members of the Federal Reserve System, and the Securities and Exchange Commission protects investors from fraud in the Wall Street market.

The Community Services Administration assists people with low incomes and limited ability to speak English to improve their conditions by helping them learn the language and acquire special working skills.

The National Foundation on the Arts and Humanities encourages artists everywhere in the country to develop their talents.

The Small Business Administration makes loans to small firms. It also makes loans to victims of floods and other natural disasters. It sees that small businesses get a fair share of government contracts.

All these agencies, as well as many that have not been mentioned here, have provided their good services to the American people. Their work has helped the American people, by and large, to a healthier and richer way of life.

THE VICE PRESIDENCY

John Adams, the first Vice President of the United States, called the vice presidency the most insignificant office that man ever conceived. John Nance Garner, Franklin Roosevelt's first Vice President, was not often seen in the nation's capital. He preferred to stay home in Texas, where he had much more to occupy his time.

The only responsibilities the Constitution gives the Vice President are: (1) to be prepared to take over the presidency, if and when the President becomes too ill to continue in the office or dies; and (2) to act as the president of the Senate.

Even in the Senate his power is limited. The one thing he is empowered to do there is to cast a vote, if and when the vote of the Senators on a bill or resolution is tied.

Vice President John Tyler became President when William Henry Harrison died in office. Vice President Calvin Coolidge became President when Warren G. Harding died in office. Vice Presidents Andrew Johnson, Chester Alan Arthur, Theodore Roosevelt, and Lyndon B. Johnson all became Presidents as a result of assassinations.

Two American Vice Presidents were never elected to the Executive Office by the people of the United States. They were elected Vice Presidents by the House of Representatives, according to the regulations prescribed by the Constitution. One was Gerald R. Ford, elected when Spiro Agnew, charged with evading income taxes, resigned the vice presidency. The other was Nelson Rockefeller, who filled the vacancy in the office when Gerald R. Ford, with the resignation of Richard M. Nixon, became President.

Two men who were never elected
to office in the usual way.
Gerald R. Ford, left,
after he became President,
discusses policy with his
Vice President, Nelson Rockefeller.

In more recent years, the Vice President has generally made positive contributions to his office. Franklin D. Roosevelt had used Vice President Henry Wallace and then Vice President Harry S. Truman in war effort work during World War II. Eisenhower had Nixon preside over Cabinet meetings and the National Security Council. Kennedy gave Lyndon B. Johnson assignments overseas and called him into decision-making meetings during the Cuban crisis of 1962. Johnson used Hubert Humphrey and Ford used Rockefeller in a similar fashion. As a result of these assignments, the office of the Vice President has gained considerable prestige both at home and abroad.

Generally, the person nominated for the presidency selects his running mate. And generally, when he makes his selection for the Vice President, he chooses someone he thinks will help the election campaign.

Franklin D. Roosevelt did not choose John Nance Garner as his running mate because he respected the man for his brilliance or his ability. Roosevelt was from the northeastern section of the country. Garner was from Texas. Roosevelt hoped that Garner would help get him the vote of the southern and southwestern states.

Similarly, when he ran a third time for office, Roosevelt chose Henry Wallace as his running mate. Roosevelt was considered a representative of the industrial East. Wallace was a man of the farming areas of the country.

To Jimmy Carter's credit, Vice President Walter Mondale was a very active Vice President. Mondale was delegated a variety of assignments, both foreign and domestic. He was also an active participant in important presidential decision making.

This does not ensure the importance of the office for future Vice Presidents. The significance of the office is still to be measured by the manner in which the Chief Executive chooses to use it.

[57]

POWER AND THE PRESIDENCY

The Founding Fathers created a government of three branches: the executive, the legislative (Congress), and the judiciary (Supreme Court). Each branch was given specific powers. Congress was to be responsible for, among other things, the enactment of laws. The President was to be responsible for, among other things, the signing of the acts of Congress, making those acts the law of the land. The Supreme Court was to be responsible for deciding, when the situation arose, whether those laws were Constitutional or not.

It was the intention of the Founding Fathers that no branch of the Government be more powerful than the others. Each branch was expected to check on the actions of the others so that there would be a balance of power among all three of them. That is why the Government of the United States is called a government of checks and balances.

For the most part, this system has worked remarkably well. While at times, Congress has been the leading power in the Government and, at other times, the President has been dominant, the Supreme Court has carried out its function of guarding the Constitution without interruption. Only once was there an effort to weaken the power of the Supreme Court, when Franklin Roosevelt proposed to increase the number of its judges with his own appointees in order to create a Court that would approve whatever laws he had enacted. His effort, which met with convincing defeat, almost lost him his re-election.

However, beginning with Franklin Roosevelt, for many years, as the United States became the leading world power, the role of the President became more and more dominant. The

[58]

*While Vice President Mondale,
members of Congress, and others watch,
President Carter signs
the Nuclear Non-Proliferation Act in 1978.*

President became not only the most powerful person in the U.S. Government, but the leader of the Free World as well.

For most people, at home and abroad, it was the President alone who spoke for the country. His opinions were considered the opinions of all America. His actions were considered the actions of the entire country. As for Congress, for many years it neglected or gave up the powers it was given by the Constitution and depended almost completely on the President for guidance and leadership.

In more recent years, however, there has been a "revolt" in Congress, which began to reclaim the powers with which it had been endowed by the Constitution. The War Measures Act was the result of this revolt. The attacks on the FBI and the CIA by Congress provide other evidence of this changing attitude.

Congress has undoubtedly regained much of its power in recent years, but, without question, the Presidency has become the most powerful branch of the Government. The position of the United States in foreign affairs has made the President, who is most responsible for foreign affairs, a dominant world figure. The economic and military strength of the United States, for which the President is primarily responsible, has made the Chief Executive perhaps the most powerful leader in the entire world.

The American people are fully aware of the position of their President in world politics. They are also fully aware of his responsibilities to the world at large, and particularly to the Free World. His position has demanded their respect and faith. The faith in the President gives the Chief Executive that much more responsibility to prove that the faith of the people is well placed; it also provides him, generally, with the overwhelming support of the people in whatever power struggle he may have with Congress. For all the checks and balances, the Executive Branch of the government is undoubtedly the most powerful branch of the Government of the United States.

FOR FURTHER READING

Cooke, Donald E. *Atlas of the Presidents* (Rev. Ed.). New Jersey: Hammond Inc., 1976.

Coy, Harold. *The First Book of the Presidents* (Updated Edition). New York: Franklin Watts, 1981.

Feerick, John and Amalie F. *The Vice-Presidents of the United States* (Updated Ed.). New York: Franklin Watts, 1981.

Johnson, Gerald W. *The Presidency*. New York: William Morrow, 1962.

Parker, Nancy W. *The President's Cabinet*. New York: Parents' Magazine Press, 1978.

Turner, Mina. *United States Government*. Boston: Houghton Mifflin, 1947.

INDEX

Adams, John, 55
Adams, Sherman, 35
Arthur, Chester Alan, 55
Assistant to the President for Domestic Affairs and Policy, 31
Assistant to the President for National Security Affairs, 31, 33

Brzezinski, Zbigniew, 46

Cabinet, 40–44
Carter, Jimmy, 18, 35, 46
Central Intelligence Agency (CIA), 38–39, 60
Coolidge, Calvin, 55

Departments, governmental
    Agriculture, 51
    Commerce, 51
    Defense, 46–47
    Education, 53
    Energy, 51
    Health and Human Services, 52
    Housing and Urban Development, 52
    Interior, 52
    Justice, 48–50
    Labor, 52
    State, 45–46
    Transportation, 53
    Treasury, 50
Dulles, John Foster, 46

Ehrlichman, John, 33
Eisenhower, Dwight D., 31, 35, 46, 51
Electoral procedures, 7–10

Executive Offices of the President
    Administration, 40
    Council of Economic Advisors, 39
    Council of Environmental Quality, 40
    Council on Wage and Price Stability, 40
    Domestic Policy Staff, 39–40
    Management and Budget, 36–38
    National Security Council, 38–39
    Science and Technology Policy, 40
    Special Representative for Trade Negotiations, 40
Executive privilege, 26–27

Federal Bureau of Investigation (FBI), 27, 39, 48–50, 60
Ford, Gerald R., 18, 20, 35, 55, 57
Frederick Augustus, Duke of York, 4

Garner, John Nance, 55, 57
George III, King of England, 4
Grant, Ulysses S., 25

Haldeman, H. R., 33
Hamilton, Alexander, 5, 42
Harding, Warren G., 44, 46, 55
Harrison, Henry, 55
Hay, John, 46
Hoover, J. Edgar, 49
Hughes, Charles Evans, 46
Hull, Cordell, 45
Humphrey, Hubert, 57

Impeachment, 12, 13–15
Impoundment of funds, 25–26

Independent agencies, 53–54
Internal Revenue Service (IRS), 50

Jackson, Andrew, 44
Jefferson, Thomas, 13, 25, 42, 44
Johnson, Andrew, 15, 55
Johnson, Lyndon B., 17, 27, 31, 35, 44, 55, 57

Kennedy, John F., 17, 27, 31, 44, 57
Kissinger, Henry, 33, 44, 45

Lance, Bert, 35
Legislation and presidential power, 23–26
Lincoln, Abraham, 15, 16, 17, 44

McKinley, William, 21, 29
Madison, James, 42, 44
Marshall, George, 46
Mondale, Walter, 57
Monroe, James, 21, 42, 44
Muskie, Edmund S., 46

Nixon, Richard M., 15, 17, 18, 20, 25–27, 31, 35, 44, 46, 55, 57

Presidential elegibility and terms of office, 10–13

Presidential power and responsibility, 1, 3–7, 16–29, 58–61

Rockefeller, Nelson, 55, 57
Rogers, William, 45
Roosevelt, Franklin D., 3, 13, 25, 27–29, 31, 44, 45, 57, 58
Roosevelt, Theodore, 23, 46, 55
Root, Elihu, 46
Rusk, Dean, 33

Secret Service, 50
Seward, William H., 45
Stanton, Edwin M., 15

Treaties and presidential power, 20
Truman, Harry S., 25, 31, 46, 57
Tyler, John, 55

Van Buren, Martin, 42
Vance, Cyrus, 46
Veto power, 25–26
Vice-Presidency, 10, 55–57

Wallace, Henry, 57
War Powers Act (1973), 17, 18, 60
War and presidential power, 16–20
Washington, George, 7, 13, 16, 29, 42, 44
White House staff, 29–35
Wilson, Woodrow, 21